The subject m
vocabulary ha

with expert assistance, and the brief and simple text is printed in large, clear type.

Children's questions are anticipated and facts presented in a logical sequence. Where possible, the books show what happened in the past and what is relevant today.

Special artwork has been commissioned to set a standard rarely seen in books for this reading age and at this price.

Full-colour illustrations are on all 48 pages to give maximum impact and provide the extra enrichment that is the aim of all Ladybird Leaders.

A Ladybird Leader

ducks and swans

written and illustrated by John Leigh-Pemberton

Publishers: Ladybird Books Ltd . Loughborough

Printed in England

Ducks and drakes

Ducks live near water.

The female is called a duck, and the male a drake.

However, both are usually known as ducks.

The babies are called ducklings.

0 7214 0365 4

The drake has brightly coloured feathers.
The duck's feathers are rather dull.

Mallard drake and duck

Surface-feeding ducks

Ducks are found all over the world.
Some feed on the surface of the water.
Some dive for their food.

What they eat

These are drakes of several kinds of surface-feeding ducks.
They eat weed, worms, frogs and insects.

Where they live

Ducks live on ponds and rivers.
Some live on lakes or the sea.
They feed and rest on land
and on the water.

Shelduck
a seaside duck

Some ducks live on farms.
They give us eggs and meat.

Feathers

Ducks have soft feathers
to keep them warm (a),
and stiff ones for flying. (b)
These are called their plumage.

(b)

(a)

(c)

Seen through a magnifying glass

Feathers are made of thousands of tiny strips of something rather like skin. (c)

Ducks comb their feathers with their beaks.
They also oil them with oil from a special gland.
This is called preening.

Gadwall

Floating

All ducks can swim.
To help them float
they have hollow bones.
Their breast-bones are shaped
like the bottom of a boat.

The feathers of ducks are waterproof. The duck stays warm and dry, and can sleep or feed as it floats.

arganey
(drake)

Feet

Ducks have four toes on each foot.
Three big toes face forwards.
One small toe faces backwards.
Each toe has a nail.

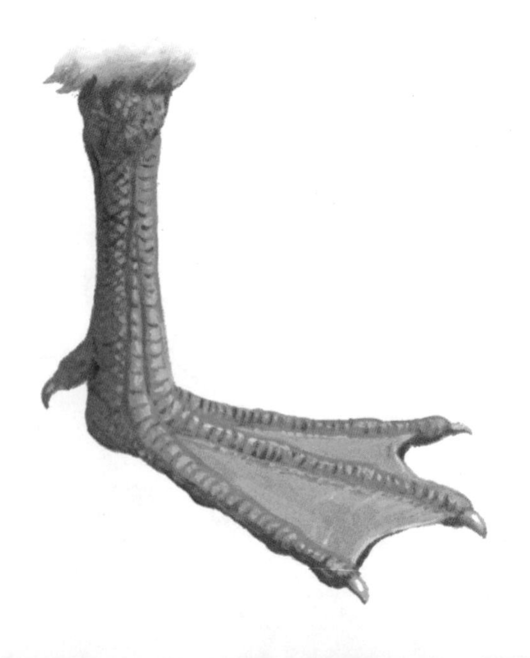

The big toes are joined by flaps of skin.
These are called webs.
Webbed feet are used like paddles
for swimming.

Up-ending

Surface-feeding ducks often feed by dipping their heads under water. This is called up-ending. They collect weed, snails and water insects.

Swimming and walking

Ducks swim easily by paddling
with their feet.

Their webbed feet help them to walk
on soft mud.

On land they walk quite well.

Voice

Ducks make many different sounds.

They call to each other or cry out when frightened.

Only the females give the loud 'quack' noise.

Female Teal

Most ducks live together
in large flocks.

Flying

The wings of ducks are made mostly of stiff feathers.

All the feathers overlap each other.

This makes the wing very strong.

A mallard's wing

Flying

Ducks fly by beating their wings quickly up and down.

They can twist their wings to help them turn in flight.

Taking off

Surface-feeding ducks take off from the water very quickly.

They can rise straight up into the air.

Teal taking off

Landing

When landing, ducks spread their wings and tails to act as brakes. They land feet first, folding their wings as they settle.

Mallard landing

Nests

Most ducks make their nests on the ground, often some way from water.

Nests are made of grass and are lined with soft feathers.

Shoveller

Eggs

Ducks lay from six to twelve eggs.
They are plain-coloured,
never spotted.
Only the female sits on the eggs
to hatch them.

Wigeon

Baby ducks

The mother duck sits on her eggs
to keep them warm.
In three or four weeks the ducklings
hatch out.
This is called the incubation period.

Soon after they hatch, the duck leads the ducklings to the water. They can swim and feed themselves at once.

A few weeks later they can fly.

Garganey (duck)

The moult

Every year, ducks lose their feathers and grow new ones.

This is called moulting and takes about four months.

For part of this time the bird cannot fly.

The eclipse

When drakes moult they lose their bright plumage and look like females.

This is called the eclipse period.

Females moult about a month later.

Shovellers

Migration

Every autumn some ducks, like these, fly from countries where the winters are cold.

They fly to a warmer land.

They return in the spring.

Golden-eye

Other ducks, like these, breed in cold countries.

They fly to warmer lands for the winter.

This travelling is called migration.

Diving ducks

Diving ducks, like these tufted ducks, feed by diving to the bottom of the water.

They can stay under for about half a minute.

Tufted ducks are often seen on park lakes.

Diving ducks, like this golden-eye drake, eat shell-fish, crabs and water plants.

Their wings and feet help them to dive.

Nests of diving ducks

Diving ducks make large nests.

These are thickly lined with small, fluffy feathers.

This is called 'down'.

It is plucked from the duck's breast.

Pochard (duck)

Eggs of diving ducks

The eggs of diving ducks are mostly greenish in colour.

Sometimes as many as fifteen are laid.

The eggs in the nest are called a 'clutch'.

Eider (duck)

Diving ducks—where they live

These are the ducks and drakes of different kinds of diving ducks.

Some of them live on the sea and others on large lakes.

Some fly from cold countries to spend the winter in warmer lands.

Others stay to nest in spring.

A few stay all the year round.

Sawbill ducks

These ducks eat fish.
The edges of their beaks have rows of points like a saw.
With these they catch and hold their food.

This sawbill is a goosander.

It nests in holes in trees.

When they are hatched, the ducklings have to scramble down to the ground.

Perching ducks

Many kinds of ducks have been brought from foreign countries. Some escape and live as wild birds. Some perching ducks are shown here.

Carolina duck
(America)

Mandarin drake and duck
(Asia and Japan)

Perching ducks spend much time in trees, and build their nests there. They like to live near ponds or lakes surrounded by woods.

Bills (or beaks)

Different kinds of ducks have different kinds of bills.

This is because of the different kinds of food they eat.

Mallard
A bill for feeding just below the surface.

Shoveller
A huge bill for 'dabbling' on the surface.

Shelduck
A bill for surface-feeding.

Wigeon
A very small bill for surface-feeding.

Goosander
A narrow bill with edges like a saw.

Wing-spots

Many surface-feeding ducks have a brightly coloured patch on their wings.

This is called a wing-spot or speculum.

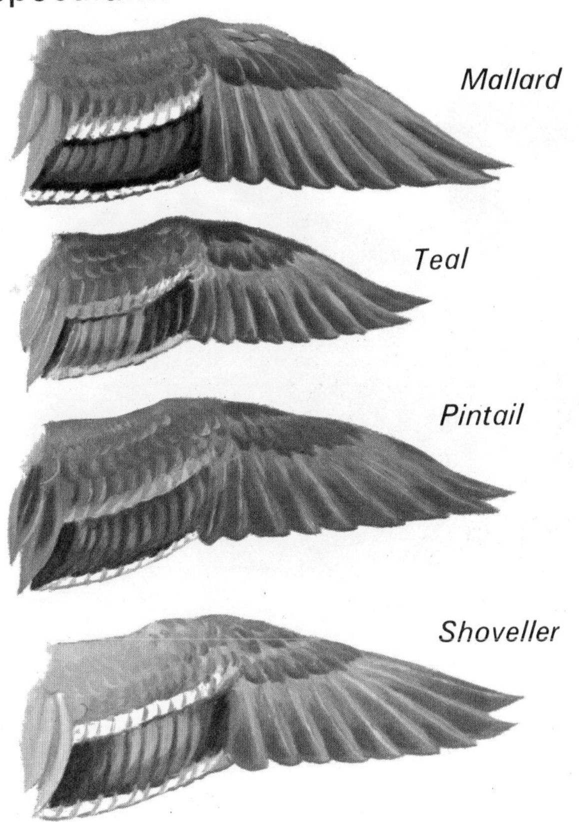

Swans

Swans are large, powerful birds.

They live on shallow water in lakes, rivers and ponds.

They are found in many parts of the world.

This is the Australian black swan.

Swans feed on water plants, frogs and worms.

They 'up-end' like some ducks.

The male is called a cob and the female a pen.

Mute swans

Swans flying

Swans are very strong fliers.
They fly with their necks stretched out and their feet tucked up behind.

Their slow, steady wing-beats make a throbbing sound which can be heard a long way off.

Swans' nests and eggs

Swans lay five or six eggs in a huge nest built of reeds, sticks and water weeds.

They like to nest near water, often on an island.

Both the pen and the cob sit on the eggs, which take thirty-five days to hatch.

The nest is fiercely guarded by the cob.

Baby swans

Baby swans are called cygnets.
They can swim and feed themselves the day after they are hatched.
In four and a half months they can fly.

Many kinds of ducks and swans
quickly become tame.
They are often kept on lakes or ponds
in town parks.

The ducks in this book